Outrageous Expressions

About the Author

Martin Jones lives in the West Country with his wife Racheal. They have a son, Lee. Martin works as an independent financial advisor. He has been collecting humorous sayings and putdowns for many years.

Outrageous Expressions

Witty, offensive and downright vulgar
turns of phrase for all occasions

!!!

Compiled by
Martin Jones

Michael O'Mara Humour

First published in Great Britain in 2000 by
Michael O'Mara Books Limited
9 Lion Yard, Tremadoc Road
London SW4 7NQ

A CIP catalogue record for this book
is available from the British Library

ISBN 1-85479-556-2

1 3 5 7 9 10 8 6 4 2

Designed and typeset by Martin Bristow

Printed and bound in Great Britain
by Cox & Wyman Ltd, Reading, Berks

!!!

I would like to dedicate this book
to all my family, friends and
acquaintances who have unwittingly
supplied me with a stream of
material for this compilation.
To my wife Racheal and son Lee,
my brother Kevin (who would forget
his balls if he didn't have them in a
bag), his wife Sandra and son
Richard. To my mother Stella and
to the outlaws Eddie and Lena.
But most of all to my late father,
Maurice 'Sally' Jones, who had the
wonderful ability to make me and
those around him laugh like drains
with his funny sayings and practical
jokes. He is greatly missed.

OUTRAGEOUS!

CONTENTS

on being Angry

He looks stonier
than a biblical execution

She's angrier than a bear
with a sore head

As savage as a meatfly

on Awkwardness

It was that awkward that I felt
like a bastard on Father's Day

I felt as out of place as a pork chop
in a synagogue

I felt like a spare prick
at a prostitute's wedding

on bad Beer

It tastes like gnats' piss

It tastes like the contents
of a rat's bladder

This pint's like weasel piss drained
through a mouldy Balaclava helmet

on bad Bods

She's got a body like a condom
full of conkers

I've seen better bodies
in a car-breaker's yard

He's built like a brick shithouse

on bad Boobs

She's got tits like spaniels' ears

She's got nipples like tax discs

Her boobs are like a photo finish
in a Zeppelin race

on bloody Boring

I'm as bored as a pacifist's pistol

This party is as flat as a witch's tit

I've seen more life in a tramp's vest

on bad Bums

Her arse wobbles like two boys
fighting under a blanket

Her arse looks like two ferrets
fighting in a sack

You can park a motorbike on that bum

on Campness

He's as camp as a row of tents

He's as bent as a butcher's hook

He's as bent as a nine-bob note

on Chat-ups

You must have a mirror in your knickers because I can see myself in them

Fancy a shag? No? Do you mind lying down while I have one?

Do you want to go halves on a bastard?

Your eyes are like spanners – when
I look into them my nuts tighten

How would you like to see the soles
of your shoes in the wing-mirrors
of my car?

How would you like your eggs in the
morning – fertilized or unfertilized?

on Class
(or lack of it)

She's got as much class
as torn wallpaper

She's lower than a halibut's nipples

She looks like a million dollars
– all green and wrinkly

on Cold

It was so cold that we bumped into
a brass monkey looking for a welder

It's colder than an Eskimo's chuff

It's colder than a nun's fanny

It's colder than a penguin's bollocks

It's colder than a grave-digger's bum

It was so cold that the one-armed
bandit in the pub had a glove on

on being Confused

As baffled as Adam on Mother's Day

As confused as a blind lesbian
in a fish-market

As confused as a fart
in a perfume factory

on being
Conspicuous

She stuck out like a bulldog's bollocks
on a budgie

on being Cooool!

He's that cool he runs night-classes
for cucumbers

on being Dirty-minded

He's got a mind like the contents of
a plain brown envelope

She's got a mind like untreated sewage

on Dress Sense (or lack of it)

I've seen wounds better dressed
than him

He's so scruffy he makes the
Turin Shroud look smart

He wore a shirt with colours so loud it
would have made Stevie Wonder blink

He's so badly dressed he looks like
an advert for Oxfam

I've seen crabs better dressed than her

She's dressed up like a dog's dinner

on being Drunk

She's as pissed as an upright mattress

As pissed as a fart
in a vacuum chamber

He's as pissed as a handcart

on Ears

You could swat flies with those ears

His ears are so big he looks like a taxi
with the doors open

He's got ears like a hatstand

on Embarrassment

She's gone pinker than a salmon's pink bits

He's as red as an overdrawn account at a blood bank

His face is redder than a smacked bum

on being Engaged

She's been engaged more times than
a British Telecom switchboard

She caught her husband-to-be like a
fish – she just wiggled her bait

He broke off the engagement because
she wanted to go too far – she wanted
to get married

on Entertainment

I've seen a better film on teeth

I've seen better bands on a cigar

It's about as entertaining
as a funfair at a funeral

on Eyes

I love your red shirt – it matches
your eyes

She's as blind as
a mole in a London fog

Your eyes are like pools of piss

Her eyes are redder than
a Communist Party tablecloth

His eyes were like piss-holes
in the snow

Your eyes are like pools –
sunken and watery

on Faces

I've seen a healthier-looking face
on a pirate flag

She's got a face like a busted sofa

His face is spottier
than a Dalmatian with acne

She's got more chins than
a Chinese telephone directory

He's got a face as long as
an undertaker's tape measure

She's got a face like a road accident

He's got a face
like a squeezed tea-bag

She's got a face like fried haddock

He's got a face
like a bulldog licking piss
off a stinging nettle

She's got a face
like a bag of greasy spanners

She's got a face
like a window-cleaner's sponge

He's got a face that looks like it's been
set on fire and put out with a cricket bat

She's got a face like a picture
– it needs hanging

They've got a picture of him in the
local hospital – it saves using
a stomach pump

She's got a face like a franked stamp

He looks like he's dunked his face
in a blender

The last time I saw something that
resembled a face like that, it was
being wiped

He's got a face like a robber's dog

on being Fat

She's so fat she looks like a Viking ship
in full sail

I wouldn't say she was fat but she
used to be a decoy for a whaling ship

You can park a car in the shadow
of his arse

He's so fat I bet he has his
own postcode

She was that fat that if you wanted to
make love to her you had to roll her in
sawdust and search for the damp patch

She's so fat she has to shove one of
her tits up the chimney just to enter
the living-room

on Feet

He's got feet so big he can stamp out
Australian bushfires

That's not shoes on his feet – it's
the boxes they came in

Are those your own feet or are you
breaking them in for a duck?

on being Follically-challenged

He's as bald as a badger's arse

I've seen more hair on a billiard ball

He's bald as a baby's bum

on Food

That steak's so big
you could almost milk it

I've tasted better chips left down
the back of the sofa

That breakfast looks like leftovers
from the organ donor clinic

on Football

He's missed the ball more times
than Cinderella

A tea-bag stays in the Cup longer

They train in Woolworths every week –
it gets them used to playing
in front of a crowd

On Forgetfulness

He was that forgetful his mother used
to wrap his school lunch in a road-map

He'd forget his bollocks if he didn't
keep them in a bag

She would forget her fanny
if it wasn't nailed to her arse

on being Fun (not)

This party is as much fun as
a fire in an orphanage

This is as much fun as pissing
on spark-plugs

It's not so much a barrel of laughs
as a vat of vomit

on Golf

He's got a swing like an octopus
putting up a deckchair

He's got a swing like a caveman
killing his lunch

Her swing was so bad that she couldn't
hit a cow's arse with a banjo

He hit the ball so straight he had to
lean sideways to see the flag

The ball landed like a butterfly
with sore feet

He's got a swing like someone killing
a snake in a phonebox

on being Hairy

She's got armpits
like a pair of Davy Crockett hats

She's got half the Black Forest
hanging out of her armpits

He's so hairy you could knit him into
a pair of gloves

on Hands (also applicable for card games)

I've seen better hands on a clock

! ! !

I've seen better hands on a leper

On Happiness

He was purring like a tomcat
having his bollocks scratched

He's as happy as a pig in shit

As happy as a dog with two dicks

on Health

He takes so many pills that when he walks he sounds like a pair of maracas

He's spent so much time drinking other people's health he's ruined his own

She's as fit as a butcher's dog

On being Horny

He's so horny that the crack of dawn
had better be careful

I'm feeling hornier
than a Viking's helmet

She was so horny she looked as if she
could suck the colour out of a marble

on being Hot

It's hot as a docker's armpit

It's as hot as a marathon runner's
jock-strap

I am so hot I could incubate chickens
in my armpits

on Hunger

I'm so hungry my stomach thinks
my throat has been cut

I'm that hungry I could eat a baby's
bum through the back of a cane chair

I'm so hungry I could eat the crotch
from a low-flying duck

On being Hung-over

I awoke with a mouth
like a wrestler's jock-strap

He's got a hangover
the size of the Isle of Man

My mouth tastes like
the bottom of a budgie's cage

on Innocence

Whiter than a pair
of Snow White's knickers

She was so innocent
she thought bollocks
were young cows

on Interesting (not)

About as interesting
as watching a scab form

I've had more fun drinking
cough mixture in a launderette

She's about as interesting
as yesterday's shit

on Legs

The last time I saw legs like that,
one of them had a message tied to it

She's got a nice pair of legs,
especially the left one

She was so bow-legged she couldn't
stop a pig in an alleyway

on Lips

She's got lips like two red slugs
fighting in a bag of flour

!!!

I always know when he is lying
– his lips move

!!!

His lips give better suction
than a vacuum cleaner

on Making it happen (not)

You have more chance of finding
a vegetarian pit-bull terrier

Your chances are not so much slim
as anorexic

You have more chance
of sprouting another dick

on Mouthiness

He's so mouthy he needs shagging
with a ragman's trumpet

If she had any more mouth
she wouldn't have any face left to wash

She never learned to swim –
she couldn't keep her mouth shut
long enough

He talks more cock
than a cartload of hens

I wonder what she will use for a mouth
when the gorilla wants his arsehole
back

She's got a gob on her like
the Mersey Tunnel

on Muscles

She's got arms like a gibbon

He's got arms like Popeye

He's so butch
his muscles have got muscles

on Necks

I've got a throat
like one of Gandhi's flip-flops

Her neck is like a dinosaur's ballbag

He's got more neck than a giraffe

on Nervousness

He's as nervous as a turkey
at Christmas

She's more nervous than a long-tailed
dog in a room full of rocking-chairs

He's so seedy he gets nervous
near a budgie's cage

on Noise

He's as noisy as a skeleton
wanking on a tin roof

She makes more noise
than a monsoon whistling up
an aardvark's arsehole

on Noses

He's got a nose
like a blind cobbler's thumb

!!!

He's got a nose
like the end of a sawn-off shotgun

!!!

If I said her nose was shorter than
Pinocchio's I'd be lying

on Obnoxious people

He's that obnoxious that I wouldn't piss
in his pocket if his balls were on fire

She needs the rough end of a pineapple
shoved up her arse

!!!

He needs a quick run-through
with a Christmas tree

!!!

I wish he would shove a rabbit
up his arse, strap a ferret to his dick
and then f**k himself

on Old people

He's so old that he can remember
when Moby Dick was a tadpole

She's so old that she can remember
when the Dead Sea was only ill

She's so old that her birthday cake
looks like a bushfire

He's so old he can remember when
Madam Butterfly was a caterpillar

He's so old his bones creak
like a ghost ship

She's got more wrinkles
than an elephant's trunk

on the Penis

He's got a dick like a baby's arm
holding an orange

He's got a dick like a turkey
poking its head through a bush

He's got a dick so big
it's got its own heart and lungs

on Periods

She's like a tramp's overcoat
– always on

She's so hot-tempered you'd think
someone lit the fuse on her tampon

She woke up this morning with a bed
like a butcher's slab

on Prudishness

She's such a prude that at school
she refused to do improper fractions

on Quietness

It is that quiet you could hear a gnat fart

I've heard a tortoise fart louder

As silent as an angel's fart

on Rarity

That car's as rare as rocking-horse shit

As rare as an Essex virgin

As rare as a brass monkey's bollocks

on Secretions

She was that excited
she slipped off the chair

Her nose is snottier
than a frog in a liquidizer

His ears are so waxy you could
stick a wick in and light them

on Sex

As much fun as pushing a
marshmallow into a slot-machine

Sex with her is as much fun as kicking
a sausage through the Albert Hall

Sex with her is like throwing your kitbag
up the highstreet

She's as crap a fit as a baguette shoved
up the Channel Tunnel

If brevity is the soul of wit, your penis
must be a riot

The Venus de Milo gives better hand
jobs than she does

on being Short

He's so short he'd drown by the time
he realized it was raining

She's so short she doesn't know if she
has a headache or her corns hurt

He's so short if he pulled his socks up
he'd be blindfolded

on being Sick

He's gone greener than frog-shit

He's just said hello to God on the big
white telephone

She's just made a pavement pizza

on Slappers

She's had more pricks than a
second-hand dartboard

She's seen more ceilings
than Michelangelo

She's kissed so many sailors her lips
move in and out with the tide

She's got so many children she's
multiplying quicker than a pocket
calculator

Her jeans are so tight you can tell if her
small change is heads or tails

They call her radio station because
she's easy to pick up – especially at
night

on being Slow

He is that slow he was three years old
before he got a birthmark

I've seen glaciers move faster than her

He trod on a snail the other day
because it was following him around –
there were two snails actually but
the other one got away

on Smelliness

This room smells like the place where
haddock go to die

It smells more fishy
than Lady Godiva's saddle

It's smellier than an anchovy on heat

on Smiling

She's got a smile like a ripple
in a slop bucket

She's got a smile like a crocodile
with wind

He's got a grin like a split watermelon

on being Speedy

He disappeared like a fart going through
a pair of string underpants

She scarpered quicker than shit
off a shovel

He was out of here faster than
a rat up a drainpipe

on being bloody Stupid

He checked out of Hotel Brainy
some years ago

She's a result short
of a classified round-up

He's one tit short of an udder

on being Subtle (not)

As subtle as a flying brick

She's as subtle as a battleship

Subtle as a gynaecologist
wearing a gas mask

on Sweating

He's sweating like a prisoner of war

She's sweating
like a pig in a bacon factory

They're sweating
like turkeys on Christmas Eve

on Teeth

I've seen better teeth
in a worn-out gearbox

Her teeth stick out so much it looks like
her nose is playing the piano

Your teeth are like stars
– they come out at night

on being Thick

If he was any thicker he would
photosynthesise in sunlight

He's ten pence short of a pound

She's a dolly mixture short of a quarter

He's thick as a donkey's dangler

She's a pork pie short of a picnic

He's got a rip in his marble bag

She's got a tile loose

She hasn't got both hands on the steering wheel

When you look into his eyes you can see that there is no one driving

She's stepped off the pavement

Lights on, door open, nobody in

Trying to explain something to him
is like trying to give a fish a bath

He'll be doing joined up writing next

He's wired up to the moon

She's like the Venus de Milo – very
beautiful but not all there

He doesn't know the meaning of the word fear. In fact he doesn't know the meaning of lots of words

He's one putt short of a par

If she went to a mind-reader they wouldn't bother charging

on being Thin

If he was thinner he would only have
one eye

She's as thin as a chicken's lip

He was that thin he looked like a
one-iron with ears

on being Tight-fisted

He's as tight as a duck's arse – and that's waterproof

He's tighter than an Italian tenor's trousers

As tight as a camel's arse in a sandstorm

He's so tight-fisted that the only way to get a drink out of him is to stick two fingers down his throat

She's so tight-fisted that instead of using deodorant she gargles disinfectant and licks her armpits

He's so tight-fisted that when he takes a ten-pound note from his wallet the Queen blinks at the light

on Tongues

Her tongue is like an electric eel

He talks like he's wearing a sock on
his tongue

Her tongue works so fast she could
whisk an egg with it

on being Two-faced

She can't be that two-faced otherwise
she wouldn't be wearing that one

He's that two-faced I bet he doesn't
know which face to wash in the
morning

He's got more front than Blackpool

on being Ugly

She's so ugly that she fakes orgasm
when she masturbates

He's so ugly his parents used to tie a
pork chop around his neck just to get
the dog to play with him

She's so ugly that if her face was her
fortune she would get a tax rebate

He's that ugly he's living proof that the
Indians f***ed buffalo

She's so ugly that if she walked into
a cornfield the crows would bring back
the corn they stole last year

Is that an ugly face or is your neck
being sick?

She's so ugly that six peeping toms
have committed suicide

He looks like a one-eyed budgie with
a squint

The last time I saw a face like that it
had a hook in its mouth

on being Unfit

He's puffing like a broken carthorse

Are you trying to get fit
or just having one?

The only regular exercise he gets
is stretching the truth

on being Unlucky

He's that unlucky if he was reincarnated
he'd come back as himself

He's that unlucky if he was a buffalo
he would bump into Wild Bill

I'm so unlucky that if I fell into a barrel
of cigars I would come out with
a turd in my mouth

on being Up and Down

She's been up and down more times
than a whore's drawers

She's been up and down like a bride's
nightgown

Her knickers are up and down like a
yo-yo

He's up and down more times than a
fiddler's elbow

They've had more ups and downs than
the Grand Old Duke of York

She's been up and down like a toilet
seat

on being Useful (not)

As useful as a grave robber
in a crematorium

!!!

As much use as an ashtray
on a motorbike

!!!

As useless as a carpet-fitter's ladder

!!!

As useful as a one-armed trapeze artist
with an itchy crotch

He couldn't manage a fart on a diet
of baked beans

About as much use as a one-legged cat
trying to bury a turd on a frozen lake

As much use as mudguards
on a tortoise

As much use as a one-legged man
in an arse-kicking competition

As much use as Captain Hook
at a gynaecologists' convention

As much use as a trapdoor on a lifeboat

He couldn't direct a turd down a toilet

He's that useless he couldn't tell the
difference between a pile of poop
and a pudding

on the Voice

His voice is like a chainsaw
striking a rusty nail

She's got a voice like a cat
with its throat cut

He's got a stutter like a runaway
sewing-machine

on being Welcome (not)

As welcome as a fart in a phonebox

As welcome as a turd in a
swimming-pool

As welcome as a turd in a water strike

As welcome as a hole in a lifeboat

As welcome as a tampon at an orgy

As welcome as a fart in a spacesuit

As welcome as a nut cutlet
at a cannibal banquet

As welcome as a taxman's letter

As welcome as a reggae band
at a Ku-Klux-Klan convention

on Wimps

He's so soppy he's like a big girl's blouse

She's wetter than a haddock's bathing costume

As wet as a tin of piss

on being Worthless

It's worth as much
as a chocolate fireguard

It's so worthless
it wouldn't raise a fart
at a bring-and-buy sale

OUTRAGEOUS!

Michael O'Mara Humour

If you would like more information on the full list of humour titles published by Michael O'Mara Books Limited, please contact our UK sales department by fax on (020) 7622 6956 or email us at:jokes@michaelomarabooks.com.

Titles include:

- Bitch!
- The Complete Book of Farting
- Dot On Men
- Dot On Top
- Life: An Abuser's Manual
- The Little Book of Blondes
- The Little Book of Bums
- The Little Book of Farting
- The Little Book of Magical Love Spells
- The Little Book of Pants
- The Little Book of Pants 2
- The Little Book of Revenge
- The Little Book of Stupid Men
- The Little Book of Venom
- The Little Book of Voodoo
- The Little Toilet Book
- The Nastiest Things Ever Said
- On Second Thoughts
- Strange Tails
- The Stupidest Things Ever Done
- The Stupidest Things Ever Said
- Stupid Movie Lines
- Stupid Sex
- Stupid Things Men Do
- The World's Greatest Lies
- The World's Stupidest Laws
- The World's Stupidest Signs
- Wrong!